MW00885535

Keto Recipes:

50 Amazing Low Carb Smoothies & Juices

Table of Contents

Introduction

I wish to thank and congratulate you for downloading *"Keto Smoothies & Juices: Take Your Pick From My Collection of Delightful Tasting, Healthy and Energizing Keto Beverage Recipes!"* You have taken a positive step towards making positive changes in your daily eating habits just by downloading this e-book. Taking that action shows me that you are someone who is serious about making healthy changes in your daily diet. Adding keto smoothies and juices to your daily diet is certainly going to make some healthy results in your overall health and well-being. Instead of choosing to drink sugar-filled sodas make yourself a nice glass of keto juice of your choice or a smoothie. I can guarantee you that you are going to benefit from making that healthier choice in beverages. Speaking of healthy beverage choices I would like to include the most important beverage choice out there—water—drink at least 8 glasses of water a day.

Now for those days when you are looking for a drink with a bit more flavor to it than water—then you will find some great healthy choices in my collection of keto smoothies and juices in this book. You can also expand on them by adding your own special ingredients to them to make them your own! You can use my recipes as a base to build your own special keto beverage from. I hope that you will enjoy making and drinking my collection of drinks as much as I do!

Chapter 1. Quick Overview of the Ketogenic Diet

I am assuming that you are somewhat familiar with the ketogenic diet at this point, but just in case you are not, let us take a quick review of what it is exactly before we dive into my collection of keto beverage recipes.

When looking at modern technology it has quickly evolved compared to the very slow evolution of the human metabolism. In human history's past our ancestors would hunt for meals, sometimes going days without food. This resulted in our bodies adapting by storing as much energy reserves as was possible for leaner times. The human body became extremely efficient at taking any excess energy (from food sources) and storing in the body in the form of fat. When food became scarce once again the human body could rely on taking energy from its stored fat. At these times the body would switch from using food as its main source of energy to fat reserves.

However, the human way of life changed greatly, as food was more plentiful. Excess energy is still stored as fat. With the modern way of living this has been exacerbated by humans producing foods that are loaded with carbohydrates (which are utilized more quickly by the body), this results in the lowering need of physical activity, hence the excess energy (more calories are consumed than are actually expended). This results in more energy being stored as fat.

Basically the concept of the ketogenic diet is that it takes advantage of your body's natural system that uses fat for fuel. It achieves this by switching to a diet that is a low carbohydrate diet, which your body adapts to. When it is unable to utilize the readily available source of carbohydrate that it once had, it then will turn to the existing and new stores of fat as its energy source. This process is known as a state of ketosis.

When we are on a diet that contains sufficient amounts of carbohydrates that are broken down into glucose which is used as a source of energy. However, when the carbs are restricted in the diet, our liver will start to produce ketones (also referred to as ketone bodies). The ketone bodies are transported from the liver to other tissues where they are reconverted by enzymes in our bodies to produce energy.

The ketogenic diet breaks down into the macronutrients as follows:

- Carbs: 20-50 grams per day

- Try 30 grams when you are starting out.

- Protein: 0.6-1 grams per pound (1.3-2.2 grams per kg) of body weight.

- If your level of physical activity is at a high level, go for a higher end as it will help you to retain/build your muscle.

- Fat: remaining calories from (good/healthy) fats.

Chapter 2. Collection of Keto Smoothie Recipes

1. Beet Red Velvet Smoothie
Ingredients:

- 1 teaspoon of Stevia
- 1 cup of unsweetened almond milk
- 1 tablespoon of cocoa powder
- 1/2 a beet
- 1/2 an avocado

Directions:

Place all of your ingredients into your blender except for the ice and blend until smooth. Add in your ice, and blend for an additional minute or so. Serve immediately.

Nutrition Facts (Per Serving)

Total Carbs: 18g

Fiber: 8g

Total Fat: 13g

Protein: 4g

831 W 119th street
Chicago IL
60643

2. Avocado & Coconut Smoothie
Ingredients:

- 1 teaspoon of Stevia
- 1 cup of ice
- 1 teaspoon of vanilla extract
- 1/2 cup of unsweetened almond milk
- 1/2 an avocado, sliced, pitted
- 1/4 cup of coconut milk

Directions:

Place all of your ingredients into your blender, except for the ice. Blend until smooth. Add in the ice, blending for an additional minute. Serve right away.

Nutrition Facts (Per Serving)

Total Carbs: 13g

Fiber: 9g

Total Fat: 36g

Protein: 4g

3. Mocha Coconut Frappe
Ingredients:

- 1 tablespoon of cocoa powder

- 2 tablespoons of strong black coffee, chilled

- 1/2 cup of unsweetened almond milk

- 1/2 cup of coconut milk

- 1 teaspoon of Stevia

- 1 tablespoon of unsweetened, shredded coconut

- 1 cup of ice

Directions:

Place all of the ingredients except the shredded coconut into your blender and blend until smooth. Top with the shredded coconut and enjoy!

Nutrition Facts (Per Serving)

Total Carbs: 11g

Fiber: 5g

Total Fat: 32g

Protein: 4g

4. Frosty Chocolate
Ingredients:

- 1 tablespoon of cocoa powder
- 1 cup of unsweetened almond milk
- 1 scoop of chocolate protein powder
- 2 medjool dates, pitted
- 1 cup of ice
- 1/4 teaspoon of Xanthan gum

Directions:

Place all of your ingredients into your blender except for the ice. Blend until smooth. Add in the ice and dates and blend for an additional minute. Serve right away.

Nutrition Facts (Per Serving)

Total Carbs: 15g

Fiber: 4g

Total Fat: 6g

Protein: 24g

5. Minty Keto Smoothie
Ingredients:

- 1 cup of unsweetened almond milk

- 1 scoop of vanilla protein powder

- 1/2 an avocado

- 1/2 a teaspoon of peppermint extract

- 1 cup of spinach, fresh

- 8-10 drops liquid Stevia

- 1 cup of ice

Directions:

Place the spinach, protein powder, avocado, and milk into your blender and blend until smooth. Add in the liquid Stevia, peppermint extract and ice. Blend until smooth. Taste the smoothie and add additional Stevia if needed to suit your personal taste.

Nutrition Facts (Per Serving)

Total Carbs: 15g

Fiber: 8g

Total Fat: 25g

Fiber: 8g

Protein: 26g

6. Spicy Cinnamon Roll Smoothie

Ingredients:

- 1 scoop of vanilla protein powder
- 1 teaspoon of cinnamon
- 1/2 a teaspoon of vanilla extract
- 1 teaspoon of flax seeds, ground
- 1 teaspoon of Stevia
- 2 cups of unsweetened almond milk
- 1/2 a cup of plain yogurt
- 1 cup of ice

Directions:

Place all of the ingredients into your blender except for the ice. Blend ingredients until smooth. Add in the ice and blend for an additional minute or so until smooth. Garnish smoothie with a sprinkle of cinnamon and serve.

Nutrition Facts (Per Serving)

Total Carbs: 9g

Total Fat: 6g

Fiber: 2g

Protein: 16g

7. Chocolate & Peanut Butter Smoothie

Ingredients:

- 1 cup of unsweetened almond milk
- 1 tablespoon of peanut butter
- 1 tablespoon of cocoa powder
- 1 scoop of protein powder
- 1 cup of ice

Directions:

Place all of your ingredients into your blender, except for the ice. Blend until smooth. Add in the ice and blend for another minute or so or until smooth. Serve immediately.

Nutrition Facts (Per Serving)

Total Carbs: 12g

Fiber: 4g

Total Fat: 14g

Protein: 28g

8. Nutty Fat Bomb Smoothie

Ingredients:

- 2 tablespoons of coconut oil
- 1 cup of unsweetened almond milk
- 1 cup of canned coconut milk
- 2 tablespoons of peanut butter
- 1/2 a teaspoon of Stevia
- 1/2 teaspoon of cinnamon
- 1/2 a teaspoon of vanilla extract
- 1 cup of ice

Directions:

Place all of your ingredients into your blender, except for the ice. Blend until smooth. Add in the ice and blend for another minute or so or until smooth. Serve immediately.

Nutrition Facts (Per Serving)

Total Carbs: 11g

Fiber: 4g

Total Fat: 52g

Protein: 7g

9. Super Green Smoothie
Ingredients:

- 1 banana, frozen

- 1 cup of baby spinach

- 1 tablespoon of coconut oil

- 1 tablespoon of almond butter

- 1 teaspoon of Stevia

- 1 cup of unsweetened almond milk

- 1 cup of ice cubes

Directions:

Place all of your ingredients into your blender, except for the ice. Blend until smooth. Add in the ice and blend for another minute or so or until smooth. Serve immediately.

Nutrition Facts (Per Serving)

Total Carbs: 17g

Fiber: 4g

Total Fat: 26g

Protein: 6g

10. Mocha Smoothie
Ingredients:

- 1/2 a cup of full-fat yogurt, plain
- 1 tablespoon of cocoa powder
- 2 teaspoons of instant coffee granules
- 2 cups of unsweetened almond milk
- 1 teaspoon of Stevia
- Coconut flakes for garnish (optional)

Directions:

Place all of your ingredients into a shallow freezer-safe bowl and mix well. Place into the freezer. Every hour for 4-5 hours scrape the mixture with a fork. Once the mixture is frozen, set it out on the counter to soften a bit. Place the mixture into your blender and blend until smooth. Top with coconut flakes and serve.

Nutrition Facts (Per Serving)

Total Carbs: 15g

Fiber: 4g

Total Fat: 9g

Protein: 10g

11. Gingered Plum Smoothie
Ingredients:

- 1 small piece of fresh ginger (about 1/2 inch)
- 1 cup of frozen plum pieces
- 1/2 cup of beet, chopped, raw
- 1/2 cup of coconut milk, canned
- 1 tablespoon of coconut oil
- 1/4 teaspoon of cinnamon
- 1 tablespoon of almond butter
- 1 cup of water
- 1/2 cup of ice

Directions:

Place all of your ingredients into your blender, except for the ice. Blend until smooth. Add in the ice and blend for another minute or so or until smooth. Serve immediately.

Nutrition Facts (Per Serving)

Total Carbs: 11g

Fiber: 3g

Total Fat: 26g

Protein: 6g

12. Green Superfood Smoothie

Ingredients:

- 1 tablespoon of parsley, fresh
- 1 cup of spinach, frozen
- 1/4 cup of pineapple, frozen
- 1/4 teaspoon of ginger, freshly grated
- 1/2 an avocado
- 1 cup of water
- 1 cup of ice

Directions:

Place all of your ingredients into your blender, except for the ice. Blend until smooth. Add in the ice and blend for another minute or so or until smooth. Serve immediately.

Nutrition Facts (Per Serving)

Total Carbs: 13g

Fiber: 6g

Total Fat: 10g

Protein: 3g

13. Fat Burning Avocado Smoothie
Ingredients:

- 1/2 a kiwi fruit

- 1/2 an avocado

- 1 tablespoon of lime juice

- 1 tablespoon of heavy cream

- 1/2 cup of unsweetened almond milk

- 1/2 a cup of ice

- 1 tablespoon of chives, chopped

- dash of sea salt

Directions:

Place all of your ingredients into your blender, except for the ice. Blend until smooth. Add in the ice and blend for another minute or so or until smooth. Serve immediately.

Nutrition Facts (Per Serving)

Total Carbs: 10g

Fiber: 5g

Total Fat: 17g

Protein: 2g

14. Almond Raspberry Smoothie

Ingredients:

- 1 scoop of vanilla protein powder
- 1/2 cup of unsweetened almond milk
- 2 tablespoons of unsalted almonds
- 1/2 cup of raspberries, frozen
- toasted almond slices as garnish (optional)

Directions:

Add all of your ingredients into blender except for garnish. Blend until smooth, garnish with toasted almonds and serve.

Nutrition Facts (Per Serving)

Total Carbs: 20g

Fiber: 9g

Total Fat: 12g

Protein: 26g

15. Tropical Raspberry Smoothie
Ingredients:

- 1 cup of raspberries, frozen

- 1/2 cup of unsweetened coconut milk

- 1/4 cup of silken organic tofu

- 1 teaspoon of Stevia

- 1 cup of ice

- fresh mint as garnish (optional)

Directions:

Place all of your ingredients into blender, except the Stevia and ice. Blend until smooth. Add in the ice and Stevia and blend for an additional minute or so. Garnish smoothie with fresh mint and serve.

Nutrition Facts (Per Serving)

Total Carbs: 21g

Fiber: 11g

Total Fat: 32g

Protein: 8g

16. Strawberry Chia Smoothie
Ingredients:

- 1 tablespoon of Chia seeds

- 1/2 cup of strawberries, frozen

- 3/4 cup of unsweetened almond milk

- 1/4 cup of heavy whipping cream

- 1/2 a teaspoon of vanilla extract

- 1 tablespoon of coconut oil

- fresh strawberries as garnish (optional)

Directions:

Place all of your ingredients into your blender, except for the ice. Blend until smooth. Add in the ice and blend for another minute or so or until smooth. Serve immediately.

Nutrition Facts (Per Serving)

Total Carbs: 14g

Fiber: 7g

Total Fat: 30g

Protein: 4g

17. Pink Delight Energizing Smoothie
Ingredients:

- 1/2 a cup of avocado

- 1 cup of strawberries, frozen

- juice of 1 lemon

- 2 celery stalks, roughly chopped

- 1 tablespoon of coconut oil

- 1 1/2 cups of coconut water

- 1/2 cup of ice cubes

- fresh strawberries as garnish (optional)

Directions:

Place all of your ingredients into your blender, except for the ice. Blend until smooth. Add in the ice and blend for another minute or so or until smooth. Serve immediately.

Nutrition Facts (Per Serving)

Total Carbs: 17g

Fiber: 8g

Total Fat: 17g

Protein: 3g

18. Chocolate Strawberry Protein Smoothie

Ingredients:

- 1 scoop of chocolate protein powder
- 1 cup of strawberries, frozen
- 2 tablespoons of cocoa powder
- 2 cups of unsweetened almond milk
- 1 tablespoon of hemp seeds
- 1 tablespoon of coconut oil
- 1/4 cup of raw almonds
- Cacao nibs (optional garnish)

Directions:

Place all of your ingredients into your blender, except for the ice. Blend until smooth. Add in the ice and blend for another minute or so or until smooth. Serve immediately.

Nutrition Facts (Per Serving)

Total Carbs: 16g

Fiber: 6g

Total Fat: 20g

Protein: 17g

19. Strawberry Cheesecake Smoothie
Ingredients:

- 1/2 a cup of strawberries, frozen
- 1 teaspoon of vanilla extract
- 1 teaspoon of Stevia
- 1/2 a cup of reduced-fat cottage cheese
- 1 cup of unsweetened almond milk
- fresh strawberries as garnish (optional)
- 1 cup of ice

Directions:

Place all of your ingredients into your blender, except for the ice. Blend until smooth. Add in the ice and blend for another minute or so or until smooth. Serve immediately.

Nutrition Facts (Per Serving)

Total Carbs: 12g

Fiber: 3g

Total Fat: 5g

Protein: 16g

20. Berry Berry Green Smoothie
Ingredients:

- 1 cup of baby spinach
- 1/4 cup of blueberries, frozen
- 1/2 cup of plain Greek yogurt
- 1/2 a cup of unsweetened almond milk
- 1 cup of ice

Directions:

Place all of your ingredients into your blender, except for the ice. Blend until smooth. Add in the ice and blend for another minute or so or until smooth. Serve immediately.

Nutrition Facts (Per Serving)

Total Carbs: 12g

Total Fat: 2g

Protein: 15g

eberry Almond Smoothie
dients:

1 cup of unsweetened almond milk

- 6 unsalted almonds

- 1/4 cup of blueberries, frozen

- 2 ounces heavy whipping cream

- 1/2 scoop vanilla protein powder

- 1 teaspoon sugar-free sweetener

- fresh blueberries and toasted almonds as garnish (op-

tional)

Directions:

Place all of your ingredients into your blender, except for the ice. Blend until smooth. Add in the ice and blend for another minute or so or until smooth. Serve immediately.

Nutrition Facts (Per Serving)

Total Carbs: 13g

Fiber: 3g

Total Fat: 31g

Protein: 25g

22. Raspberry Cream Smoothie
Ingredients:

- 1/4 cup of heavy whipping cream
- 2/3 cup of raspberries, fresh or frozen
- 1 teaspoon of Stevia
- 1/2 a teaspoon of vanilla extract
- 1/4 cup of coconut cream
- 1/2 a cup of water
- 1/2 cup of ice

Directions:

Place all of your ingredients into your blender, except for the ice. Blend until smooth. Add in the ice and blend for another minute or so or until smooth. Serve immediately.

Nutrition Facts (Per Serving)

Total Carbs: 14g

Fiber: 7g

Total Fat: 40g

Protein: 3g

23. Orange Kale Smoothie

Ingredients:

- 2 scoops vanilla protein powder

- 1/2 a teaspoon Stevia

- dash of cinnamon

- dash of ginger powder

- 1 orange, peel and seeds removed

- 1 cup kale, chopped, raw

- 1 cup water

Directions:

Place all of your ingredients into your blender, except for the ice. Blend until smooth. Add in the ice and blend for another minute or so or until smooth. Serve immediately.

Nutrition Facts (Per Serving)

Total Carbs: 29g

Fiber: 5.6g

Total Fat: 0.2g

Protein: 3.8g

24. Green Pear Protein Smoothie
Ingredients:

- 2 scoops vanilla protein powder

- 1 cup unsweetened almond milk

- 1 cup spinach, chopped

- 1 pear, cored

- 1/2 teaspoon Matcha tea powder

Directions:

Place all ingredients into your blender and blend until smooth and serve.

Nutrition Facts (Per Serving)

Total Carbs: 24.3g

Fiber: 6.0g

Total Fat: 3.8g

Protein: 2.4g

25. Mango & Lime Smoothie

Ingredients:

- 2 cups collard greens

- 1 1/2 cups mango, frozen

- 2 tablespoons lime juice, fresh

- 1 cup green grapes

Directions:

Blend all of your ingredients in a blender until smooth. Add water to get the consistency you prefer.

Nutrition Facts (Per Serving)

Total Carbs: 95.8g

Fiber: 11.3g

Total Fat: 2.9g

Protein: 6.8g

26. Carrot & Ginger Smoothie
Ingredients:

- 3/4 cup carrot juice

- 1 tablespoon hemp protein powder

- 1/2 inch piece ginger, fresh

- 1/2 apple, cored

- 1/2 cup ice cubes

Directions:

Add all of your ingredients to your blender and blend until smooth and enjoy!

Nutrition Facts (Per Serving)

Total Carbs: 23.5g

Fiber: 4.7g

Total Fat: 0.2g

Protein: 1.0g

27. Key Lime Pie Smoothie
Ingredients:

- 1 cup of coconut milk

- zest and juice 2 limes

- 1/2 cup avocado

- 1 teaspoon Stevia

- 1 tablespoon hemp protein powder

- 1 cup ice

Directions:

Add all of your ingredients to your blender and mix until smooth.

Nutrition Facts (Per Serving)

Total Carbs: 19.6g

Fiber: 10.2g

Total Fat: 71.5g

Protein: 6.9g

28. Peach Coconut Smoothie
Ingredients:

- 2 large peaches, peeled, cut into chunks

- 1 cup of full fat coconut milk, chilled

- 1 tablespoon hemp protein powder

- 1 cup ice

- zest 1 lemon, to taste

Directions:

Place all ingredients into blender, until smooth and enjoy!

Nutrition Facts (Per Serving)

Total Carbs: 28.0g

Fiber: 4.6g

Total Fat: 0.8g

Protein: 2.8g

29. Strawberry Coconut Smoothie

Ingredients:

- 1 cup coconut milk

- 2 cups strawberries, frozen

- 1 banana, frozen

- 1 teaspoon vanilla extract

- 1 tablespoon hemp protein powder

Directions:

Add all of the ingredients into your blender and mix until smooth.

Nutrition Facts (Per Serving)

Total Carbs: 62.9g

Fiber: 14.1g

Total Fat: 58.5g

Protein: 8.7g

30. Pineapple & Baby Kale Smoothie
Ingredients:

- 1 tablespoon hemp protein powder

- 1 cup almond milk

- 1/2 cup pineapple, frozen

- 1 cup kale

Directions:

Add all of your ingredients to your blender, blend until smooth and serve.

Nutrition Facts (Per Serving)

Total Carbs: 31.1g

Fiber: 7.4g

Total Fat: 57.3g

Protein: 7.9g

31. Coco Orange Smoothie
Ingredients:

- 1/2 cup of coconut milk, full fat

- 1 teaspoon vanilla extract

- 1 tablespoon hemp protein powder

- 1/2 cup orange juice, fresh squeezed

- 1/2 cup crushed ice

Directions:

Place ingredients into blender adding in the ice as you need it to get the consistency that you want.

Nutrition Facts (Per Serving)

Total Carbs: 20.1g

Fiber: 2.9g

Total Fat: 28.9g

Protein: 3.6g

32. Yummy Vanilla Smoothie
Ingredients:

- 1/4 cup almond butter
- 1 cup coconut milk
- 1 tablespoon vanilla protein powder
- 1 teaspoon Stevia
- 1 teaspoon vanilla extract

Directions:

Add all of the ingredients into blender and blend until smooth.

Nutrition Facts (Per Serving)

Total Carbs: 14.6g

Fiber: 5.7g

Total Fat: 59.5g

Protein: 6.3g

33. Coconut Pineapple Deluxe Smoothie

Ingredients:

- 1 cup coconut milk
- 1 cup pineapple chunks
- 1/2 cup pineapple juice
- 1 ripe banana
- 1 teaspoon Stevia
- 1 tablespoon hemp protein powder
- 1/2 cup ice cubes

Directions:

Add to your blender all of your ingredients and blend until smooth.

Nutrition Facts (Per Serving)

Total Carbs: 78.0g

Fiber: 10.9g

Total Fat: 58.0g

Protein: 8.1g

34. Apple Smoothie
Ingredients:

- 1 cup almond milk

- 1/2 cup coconut milk

- 1 medium apple, cored, peeled

- 2 tablespoons hemp protein powder

- 2 tablespoons cashew butter

- 1/2 cup ice cubes

Directions:

Blend all of the ingredients in a blender until smooth then enjoy!

Nutrition Facts (Per Serving)

Total Carbs: 50.8g

Fiber: 13.3g

Total Fat: 86.2g

Protein: 8.8g

35. Citrus Smoothie
Ingredients:

- half a cup lemon juice

- 1 cup almond milk

- 1 tablespoon flaxseed oil

- 2 tablespoons hemp protein powder

- 1 medium orange, peeled, sliced into sections

- 1/2 cup of ice

Directions:

Place all of your ingredients into blender, except flaxseed oil. Once blended add to serving glass and stir in the flaxseed oil.

Nutrition Facts (Per Serving)

Total Carbs: 13.3g

Fiber: 5.3g

Total Fat: 71.2g

Protein: 5.5g

36. Vanilla Blueberry Smoothie
Ingredients:

- 1 cup blueberries, fresh
- 2 cups almond milk
- 1 tablespoon flaxseed oil
- 2 tablespoons hemp protein powder
- 1/2 cup ice cubes

Directions:

Blend all of the ingredients in your blender until smooth, except for the flaxseed oil. Pour mixture into a serving glass and add in the flaxseed oil and stir. Serve immediately.

Nutrition Facts (Per Serving)

Total Carbs: 47.6g

Fiber: 14.1g

Total Fat: 128.9g

Protein: 12.1g

37. Banana & Hazelnut Butter Smoothie

Ingredients:

- 1/2 cup almond milk

- 1/2 cup coconut milk

- 2 tablespoons hazelnut butter

- 1/4 banana, ripe

- 1/2 teaspoon Stevia

- 2 tablespoons hemp protein powder

- 1/2 cup ice cubes

Directions:

Add all of your ingredients into blender and blend until smooth. Serve immediately.

Nutrition Facts (Per Serving)

Total Carbs: 21.6g

Fiber: 7.0g

Total Fat: 63.0g

Protein: 7.2g

38. Blueberry Almond Smoothie
Ingredients:

- 1 cup unsweetened blueberries, frozen

- 1 cup almond milk

- 2 tablespoons hemp protein powder

- 1 tablespoon flaxseed oil, cold-pressed organic

Directions:

Place all of your ingredients into blender except for flaxseed oil. Blend until smooth. Pour into serving glass and add in flaxseed oil and stir. Serve immediately.

Nutrition Facts (Per Serving)

Total Carbs: 13.3g

Fiber: 5.3g

Total Fat: 71.2g

Protein: 5.5g

39. Chocolate Banana Smoothie

Ingredients:

- 1 cup almond milk

- 1 bananas, frozen, peeled

- 2 tablespoons hemp seed

- 1/4 teaspoon cinnamon

- 1/4 teaspoon vanilla extract

- 1 tablespoon cocoa powder

- 1/2 cup ice cubes

- 1 teaspoon Stevia

Directions:

Place all ingredients into a blender and blend until smooth. Serve immediately.

Nutrition Facts (Per Serving)

Total Carbs: 43.8g

Fiber: 10.3g

Total Fats: 58.3g

Protein: 7.8g

40. Walnut & Chocolate Delight
Ingredients:

- 30g dark chocolate, sugar-free, broken up

- 2 tablespoons hemp protein

- 50g walnuts, crushed

- 2 cups almond milk

- 1 cup ice

Directions:

Blend all ingredients together, until smooth. This recipe makes 2 smoothies.

Nutrition Facts (Per Serving)

Total Carbs: 49.4g

Fiber: 15.0g

Total Fat: 152.8g

Protein: 25.3g

Chapter 3. Collection of Keto Juice Recipes

41. Zingy Zesty Zucchini Juice
Ingredients:

- 1 cup baby spinach

- 1 medium zucchini

- 1/2 a cucumber

- 1/2 cup fresh mint leaves

- 1 nub ginger root, fresh grated

Directions:

Place all of the ingredients through your juicer and enjoy!

Nutrition Facts (Per Serving)

Total Carbs: 11g

Fiber: 4g

Total Fat: 1g

Protein: 3g

42. Zingy Pear Limeade
Ingredients:

- 1 lime, peeled

- 1/2 green pear

- 4 kale leaves, large

- 2 celery stalks

- 1 teaspoon Stevia

Directions:

Place all of your ingredients into your juicer, except for the Stevia. Juice the ingredients then pour into serving glass and in Stevia, stir, and enjoy!

Nutrition Facts (Per Serving)

Total Carbs: 14g

Fiber: 4g

Total Fat: 0g

Protein: 2g

43. Green Pineapple Juice
Ingredients:

- 1 cucumber

- 1/4 cup pineapple, cubed

- 2 celery stalks

- 3 romaine leaves, large

- 1/2 green apple

- 1 nub ginger, small, grated

Directions:

Place all of your ingredients into juicer and juice, place in the fridge for 30 minutes before serving.

Nutrition Facts (Per Serving)

Total Carbs: 12g

Fiber: 4g

Total Fat: 1g

Protein: 2g

44. Cucumber Lemonade
Ingredients:

- 4 celery stalks

- 2 lemons, peeled

- 2 cucumbers

Directions:

Run all of your ingredients through a juicer and enjoy!

Nutrition Facts (Per Serving)

Total Carbs: 19g

Fiber: 9g

Total Fat: 1g

Protein: 5g

45. Veggie-Stuffed Green Juice
Ingredients:

- 3 celery stalks
- 4 kale leaves, large
- 2 lemons, peeled
- 1 medium cucumber
- handful parsley, fresh

Directions:

Place all of the ingredients through your juicer and enjoy!

Nutrition Facts (Per Serving)

Total Carbs: 18g

Fiber: 8g

Total Fat: 1g

Protein: 6g

46. Tropical Kiwi Juice
Ingredients:

- 1 kiwi, peeled

- 1 handful mint, fresh

- 1 cup baby spinach

- 1/2 avocado

- 1 cup coconut water

- 1 cup ice

Directions:

Place all of the ingredients into your blender except for ice. Blend until smooth. Add in the ice and blend for an additional minute.

Nutrition Facts (Per Serving)

Total Carbs: 21g

Fiber: 10g

Total Fat: 20g

Protein: 4g

47. Green Grapefruit Ginger Juice

Ingredients:

- 1 piece ginger, fresh

- 1/2 grapefruit, peeled

- 1 cup spinach, fresh

- 1 handful parsley, fresh

- 1 cup water

- 1 cup ice

Directions:

Place all of your ingredients into a blender, except for ice. Blend until smooth. Add in ice and blend for an additional minute.

Nutrition Facts (Per Serving)

Total Carbs: 11g

Fiber: 2g

Total Fat: 0g

Protein: 2g

48. Pear Energy Juice
Ingredients:

- 1/2 green pear
- 1 cup baby spinach
- handful of basil, fresh
- 1/2 avocado
- 1 cup of water
- dash of cinnamon, as garnish (optional)

Directions:

Place all of your ingredients into the blender and blend until smooth. You may use additional water to reach the consistency that you are seeking. Serve right away.

Nutrition Facts (Per Serving)

Total Carbs: 18g

Fiber: 8g

Total Fat: 10g

Protein: 3g

49. Sweet Melon Delight

Ingredients:

- 1/2 of honeydew melon, cubed, about 4 cups

- 2 mint leaves, fresh

- 1/2 cup light coconut milk

- 1 teaspoon lime juice, fresh

- 1 cup ice

- 1 teaspoon Stevia, depending how sweet melon is

Directions:

Cut your melon in half, and remove the seeds, and slice away the outer rind. Cut the melon into cubes, adding them to your blender. Also add in the blender your coconut milk, mint, lime and ice. Blend until smooth. Serve with a garnish of mint leaf.

Nutrition Facts (Per Serving)

Total Carbs: 64.8g

Fiber: 7.8g

Total Fat: 29.5g

Protein: 6.2g

50. Detox Juice
Ingredients:

- 2 red apples, big, diced
- 3/4 cup filtered water
- 1 cup baby spinach
- 1 piece, ginger, small, diced, peeled
- 1/2 a teaspoon of wheatgrass powder, optional
- 1 teaspoon flax oil, optional
- 1 cup ice cubes

Directions:

Add all of your ingredients into your blender, blend until smooth and serve immediately.

Nutrition Facts (Per Serving)

Total Carbs: 62.7g

Fiber: 11.5g

Total Fat: 5.6g

Protein: 2.1g

Conclusion

I hope that you and your loved ones will enjoy using my collection of smoothie and juice recipes. Just remember that you can use these healthy recipes as a base to make your own creations in smoothies and juices. Try having some healthy fun by adding some of your own favorite ingredients to these recipes to give them that special flavor that will suit your own personal tastes. Think of how much better you are going to feel when you have had a wonderful morning smoothie or glass of juice to help get you energized and ready to meet your day. I can assure you that you will find that you have more energy to get things done when you add keto smoothies and juices into your daily diet. Who said healthy foods had to taste bad—I love all of these yummy drinks not because they are healthy but more because they taste so yummy! The healthy part is just a wonderful added bonus—start drinking your way to a healthier you today!

I just want to thank you once again for supporting my work by downloading this book. I can assure you that your kind support means a great deal to me. I would love to read a review by you of my book on Amazon. Best of luck in enjoying drinking your way to good health with keto smoothies and juices—cheers to your health!

FREE Bonus Reminder

If you have not grabbed it yet, please go ahead and download your special bonus report *"Leptin Resistance. 21 Leptin Recipes For Weight Loss & Healthy Living"*.
Simply Click the Button Below

OR **Go to This Page**
http://easyweightlossway.com/free/

BONUS #2: More Free & Discounted Books & Products
Do you want to receive more Free & Discounted Books & Products?
We have a mailing list where we send out our new Books & Products when they go free or with a discount on Amazon. Click on the link below to sign up for Free & Discount Book & Product Promotions.
=> Sign Up for Free & Discount Book & Product Promotions <=

OR Go to this URL
http://zbit.ly/1WBb1Ek

Diabetes
Fat Burn

Kevala
Organic
Coconut Butter

88778921R00035

Made in the USA
Lexington, KY
17 May 2018